Piano - Vocal - Guitar

Wedding & Love Songs

FOR A NEW CENTURY

ISBN 0-634-00521-9

HAL•LEONARD®
CORPORATION
7777 W. BLUEMOUND RD. P.O. BOX 13819 MILWAUKEE, WI 53213

Visit Hal Leonard Online at
www.halleonard.com

Wedding & Love Songs
FOR A NEW CENTURY

CONTENTS

ALWAYS

Words and Music by
JON BON JOVI

This Ro-me-o is bleed-ing,
pic-tures that you left be-hind are just

Well, there ain't no luck ___ in these

when I die ___ you'll be on my mind ___ and I'll love you,

al - ways.

Guitar solo - ad lib. and Fade

Repeat ad lib. and Fade

Lead vocal ad lib.

FOREVER AND EVER, AMEN

Words and Music by DON SCHLITZ
and PAUL OVERSTREET

MCA Music Publishing

BEAUTIFUL IN MY EYES

Words and Music by
JOSHUA KADISON

BUTTERFLY KISSES

Words and Music by RANDY THOMAS
and BOB CARLISLE

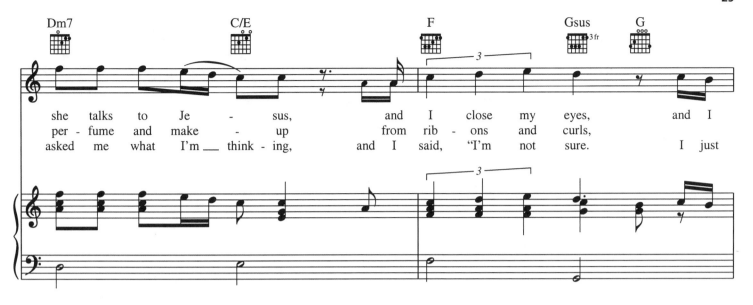

she talks to Je - sus, and I close my eyes, and I
per - fume and make - up from rib - ons and curls,
asked me what I'm ___ think - ing, and I said, "I'm not sure. I just

thank God ___ for all ___ of the joy in my ___ life.
try - ing ___ her wings out in a great big world. ___
feel like ___ I'm los - ing my ba - by girl." ___

Oh, but most of all, for but - ter - fly kiss - es ___ af - ter
But I re - mem - ber but - ter - fly kiss - es ___ af - ter
Then she leaned o - ver, gave me but - ter - fly kiss - es ___ with her

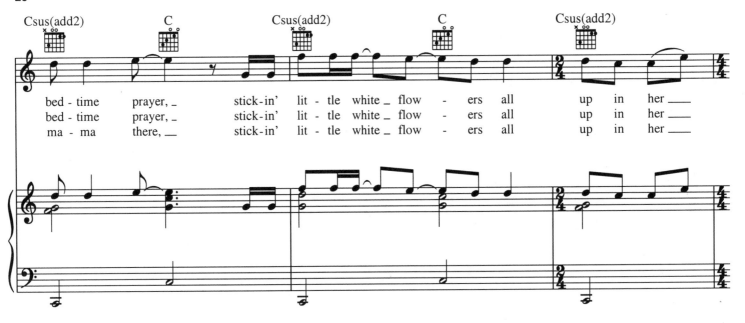

bed - time prayer, ___ stick-in' lit - tle white _ flow - ers all up in her ___
bed - time prayer, ___ stick-in' lit - tle white _ flow - ers all up in her ___
ma - ma there, ___ stick-in' lit - tle white _ flow - ers all up in her ___

hair. "Walk be - side ___ the po - ny, dad - dy, it's
hair. "You know how much ___ I love ___ you, dad - dy, but if
hair. "Walk me down ___ the aisle, ___ dad - dy, it's

my first ride. ___ I know the cake ___ looks fun - ny, dad - dy, but
you don't mind, ___ I'm on - ly goin' ___ to kiss ___ you on ___ the
just a - bout time. Does my wed - ding gown ___ look pret - ty, dad - dy? Dad -

CAN YOU FEEL THE LOVE TONIGHT

from Walt Disney Pictures' THE LION KING

Music by ELTON JOHN
Lyrics by TIM RICE

GROW OLD WITH ME

Words and Music by
JOHN LENNON

HAVE I TOLD YOU LATELY

Words and Music by
VAN MORRISON

I BELIEVE IN YOU AND ME

from the Touchstone Motion Picture THE PREACHER'S WIFE

Words and Music by DAVID WOLFERT
and SANDY LINZER

I FINALLY FOUND SOMEONE

from THE MIRROR HAS TWO FACES

Words and Music by BARBRA STREISAND, MARVIN HAMLISCH,
R.J. LANGE and BRYAN ADAMS

I'LL STILL BE LOVING YOU

Words and Music by TODD CERNEY, PAM ROSE,
MARYANN KENNEDY and PAT BUNCH

Chang-ing my life_____ with your love_____
Nev-er be-fore_____ did I know_____

has been so eas-y for_____ you._____
how lov-ing some-one could_____ be._____

And I'm a-mazed_____ ev-'ry day_____
Now I can see_____ you and

I WILL BE HERE

Words and Music by
STEVEN CURTIS CHAPMAN

IF I NEVER KNEW YOU
(Love Theme from POCAHONTAS)
from Walt Disney's POCAHONTAS

Music by ALAN MENKEN
Lyrics by STEPHEN SCHWARTZ

Male: If I nev - er knew you, ___

Female: Some - how we'd make the whole world __ bright. __ **Both:** I nev - er knew that fear and

hate could be so strong, all they'd leave us were these whis-pers in the night, ____ but

still my heart is say - ing we were right. _____ **Female:** Oh. _____

Male: There's no mo - ment I re - gret __ if I nev - er knew __

If I nev - er knew you,

IF WE FALL IN LOVE TONIGHT

Words and Music by JAMES HARRIS III
and TERRY LEWIS

IT'S YOUR LOVE

Words and Music by
STEPHONY E. SMITH

THE KEEPER OF THE STARS

Words and Music by KAREN STALEY,
DANNY MAYO and DICKEY LEE

LOVE OF A LIFETIME

Words and Music by BILL LEVERTY
and CARL SNARE

LOVE CAN BUILD A BRIDGE

Words and Music by PAUL OVERSTREET,
JOHN JARVIS and NAOMI JUDD

LOVE REMAINS

Words and Music by TOM DOUGLAS
and JIM DADDARIO

TO LOVE YOU MORE

Words and Music by JUNIOR MILES
and DAVID FOSTER

LOVE WITHOUT END, AMEN

Words and Music by
AARON G. BARKER

MY HEART WILL GO ON
(Love Theme from 'Titanic')
from the Paramount and Twentieth Century Fox Motion Picture TITANIC

Music by JAMES HORNER
Lyric by WILL JENNINGS

THE POWER OF LOVE

Words by MARY SUSAN APPLEGATE and JENNIFER RUSH
Music by CANDY DEROUGE and GUNTHER MENDE

SAVE THE BEST FOR LAST

Words and Music by PHIL GALDSTON,
JON LIND and WENDY WALDMAN

SOMETHING ABOUT
THE WAY YOU LOOK TONIGHT

Words and Music by ELTON JOHN
and BERNIE TAUPIN

There was a time ___ I was
tell you ___ how you
smile, ___ you

ev - 'ry - thing ___ and noth - ing all in ___ one. ___
light up ev - 'ry sec - ond all of the ___ day, ___
pull the deep - est se - crets from my ___ heart. ___

When you found me, ___
but in the moon - light, ___
In all hon - es - ty, ___

Original Key: F-sharp major. This edition has been transposed down one half-step to be more playable.

VALENTINE

Words and Music by JACK KUGELL
and JIM BRICKMAN

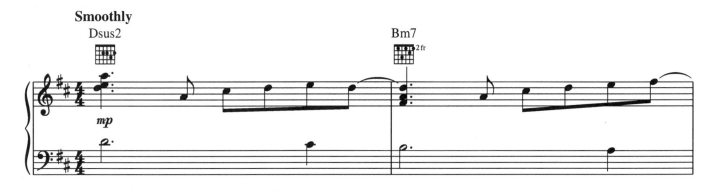

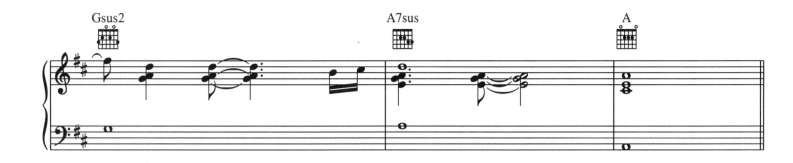

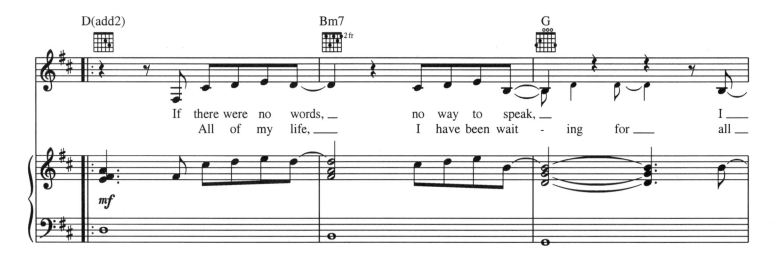

If there were no words, __ no way to speak, __ I __
All of my life, __ I have been wait - ing for __ all __

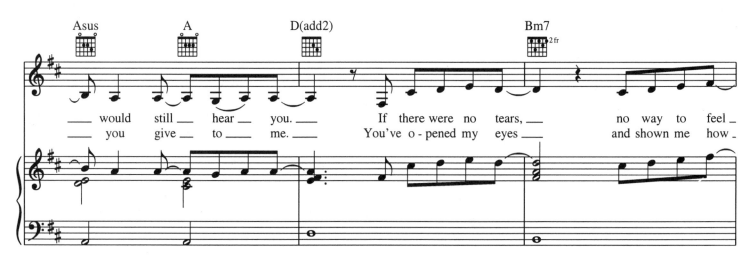

__ would still __ hear __ you. __ If there were no tears, __ no way to feel __
__ you give __ to __ me. __ You've o - pened my eyes __ and shown me how __

THE WEDDING SONG

By KENNY G
and WALTER AFANASIEFF

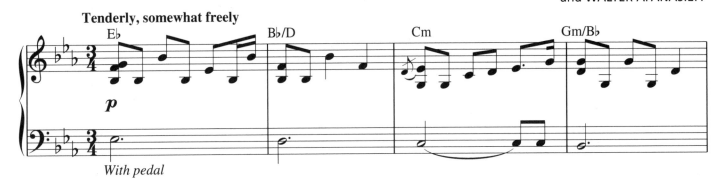

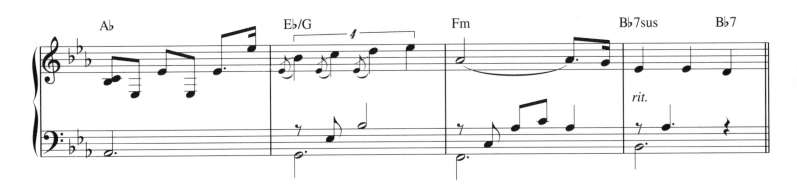

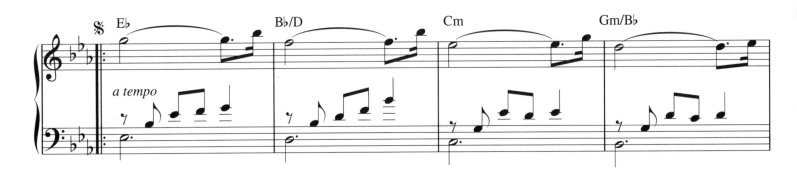

WHEN YOU SAY NOTHING AT ALL

Words and Music by DON SCHLITZ
and PAUL OVERSTREET

You Must Love Me

from the Cinergi Motion Picture EVITA

Words by TIM RICE
Music by ANDREW LLOYD WEBBER

Flowing ♩=92

1. Where do we go from here?
2. *(See additional lyrics)*

This is-n't where we in-tend-ed to be.___ We had it all,___ you be-

lieved ___ in me, ___ I be - lieved ___ in you. ___

Additional Lyrics

Verse 2: *(Instrumental 8 bars)*
Why are you at my side?
How can I be any use to you now?
Give me a chance and I'll let you see how
Nothing has changed.
Deep in my heart I'm concealing
Things that I'm longing to say,
Scared to confess what I'm feeling
Frightened you'll slip away,
You must love me.

A WHOLE NEW WORLD
(Aladdin's Theme)
from Walt Disney's ALADDIN

Music by ALAN MENKEN
Lyrics by TIM RICE

You Were Meant For Me

Words and Music by JEWEL KILCHER
and STEVE POLTZ